S O C I E T Y

Physical.
Chemistry.
Psychological.
Craving.
Persistence.
Consistence.
Pain.
Chronic.

Science.
Social science.
Society.
Social compliance.

Reject.
Inferior.
Rewired.
Irresistible.
Resistance.
Indulgence.
Rain.
Idiotic.

noun
1.
the state of being enslaved to a habit or practice or to something that is physically or psychologically habit-forming.
- *characterized by tolerance and well-established physiological symptoms upon withdrawal.*

RATS

Rats   *Rats*

Rats

Rats   *Rats*

The rat is out the cage.
The rat is in the park.
The rat is on the street.
The rat is out the dark.

DISEASE

Venomous breaths of air.
Pollution of the worst kind.
Contamination in a mask.
Virus in your mind.

It is more than that. More than what is seen by the eye. A disease,
a killer. Watch as the body will die.

Admiration for your persistence.
Not as strong as my resistance.
Willpower? You say.
I am certain I have it all.
As you will be the one to give up first.
You will be the one to fall.

JEANS

Legs seem longer in her jeans.
Will we ever know if it is in her genes?

Legs that will knock you to the floor
on her first step.

Swallowing her up.

Mastered by a pair of genes.
Overthrown by a pair of jeans.

Genetic variation.
Legalities causing inflation.

Wandering down the branch
on her lonely family tree.
Is anybody wearing the same jeans
just like the ones we can see?

AGES

Waiting for the effect.
Not the only one to face the affect.

Chaotic.
Before birth.
You are already learning.
Premature knowledge of earth.

Violence.
In education.
The drops begin to climb.
Give in to temptation.

Suffer.
Performance at work.
Attention span is failing.
Clear water turns to murk.

Neglect.
Aged before your time.
A face to tell your story.

Read
in
between
the line.

Line.

help

Line.

help

Line.

Keep writing new lines for me.
With age; the lines are blind.
Still the lines are all I see.

Slam.

There goes the door again, shit.
You can feel it; the tide sucking in and the birds flying high.
You can feel it.

The not knowing is the worst part, you just do not know. Will it just pass over and we continue in false happiness? Or will it be the stare of hatred, emptiness, death…

The eyes of alcohol.

H
O
M
E.

H elp
O dd
M ad
E ndless.

Sofa. Worn.
Blankets. Torn.
Bed. Unmade.
Lights. No shade.

Damp. Drip.
Wine. Sip.

3…2…1. The door opens, she is in. I would say she is 'home'; but home implies family and 'family' was purely a word when she was around. There she stands in all her glory; the look of sunburn on her face as alcohol pours out of her complexion. Here we fucking go again.

3…2…1… 'I HAVE HAD ENOUGH.' So, it starts; 'I WANT YOU OUT OF MY 'OUSE.'

What a delightful accent of hers.

Every word repeating like a broken record stuck on the same song playing over and over, again and again.

over and over, again and again.

over and over, again and again
over and over, again and again
over and over, again and again
over and over, again and again
over and over, again and again
over and over, again and again

PASS THE PARCEL

They played pass the parcel.
I watched pass the bottle.

But
the bottle is being passed from one hand to another.
Neither
left or right is a friend, sister or brother.
Unwrapping until emptiness.
Forgetting for forgiveness.
'I cannot remember.'
She can.
She saw.
Venom filled her veins
which passed through her eyes.

But
she saw.
Saw her daughter.
The venom passed through her eyes
as her daughter passed by her side.
The last drip of the bottle was louder than the meet with the floor.

Emptiness is the aim.
Forgetting is a claim.
Her infinite drinking game.

ROCK

Cradled
a chair
forward
backward
safety.

Protection
her arms
stand still
safe
moving gently
in place.

Ironic
the pace
now brings fear to my eye.

faster
sharp
electric
shock

Her arms now cradle the body of herself.

She is not stopping
not stopping the rocking.

The chair symbolised care.
The care is now just air.

The air, now suffocated with arms she holds.

Holding her refusal to share.

PARENT

A parent to a parent.
Carrying her to bed.
She lays lifeless on the floor.
A glass next to her head.

A scream, a cry.
Self-inflicted pain.
Waiting for the sun to rise.
To repeat all over again.

Life.
No living.
A life spent
forgiving.

Forgiving her
for giving up.
Endless pools
of tears, not enough.

Slowly
you add more.
Quickly
levels are low.

Defying
the law.
The law of diminishing returns.

Benefits will fade.
More is less.
Craving more… more… more.
Life falls to a mess.

OXYMORON

They say you are enough.
Yet they still shout there is not enough.

Less is more, so they say.
Whilst taunting there is too little.

They will scream for you to get self-respect.
Gulping down the third bottle of wine.

Do not tell me I am crazy.
Then tell me it is not my fault.

She drinks wine.
He gambles his life away.

Yet when I do not eat; I become a game that they can play.

RING

the phone is ringing
my phone is ringing

your phone is ringing
your friend is ringing

my friend is ringing
i do not care who is ringing

you do not care who is ringing
you just listen to the ringing

B
M
I
L
C   UP.

Stairs.
No lift.
An elevation in time.
No button.

NO.
stop/pause/forward/rewind.

Arch unfolded
the ground seemingly higher.

An arch now a tower.

Prominent laws from the top;
unexpected cold shower.

Birds peck away
at the structure as we climb.
Pecking the frail path
plummeting in time.

LOUDER

YOU CAN NOT HEAR THE RINGING
WHEN THE VOICES ARE SINGING
YOU ARE TRYING TO SING ALONG
YOU ARE GETTING THE WORDS WRONG
DO NOT DAR SING IT OUT LOUD
DUETS ARE NOT ALLOWED
THIS SONG IS FOR YOU
AND SOLELY FOR YOUR HEAD
WITH WORDS MUCH MORE POWERFUL
THAN ANY BOOK
YOU HAVE READ.

* * *

R E A L I T Y

Every day it is all the same.
'Hi, hello, good morning, how are you?'
Hi.
Hello.
Good morning.
How are you?
What fine weather.
Fine.
I am fine.
I said I am fine.
I'm just tired.

TIME

I wish I understood the concept of

time

Innumerable amounts.
Compact.
Close your eyes for a second.
You have lost track.

AM

A ring.
A beep.
The stop.
No sleep.

AM.
Ante Meridiem.
AM
Am I awake?

H_2O.
On my face.
Down my throat.
Still water, still awake.
A brew.
A boil.
Craving alertness.
A drink like soil.

United.
In uniform.
New face.
Same body.

Movement of the hands.
Combinations in the feet.
Small talk in the air.
The same every week.

CLOCK

We are all sat. Absolute silence.
Silence. Stillness.
Up. Down.
Watching the same arm.
To the left. Left. Left. Left.
Playing fetch with the stick.
Destined to fall.
Horizontal lines on weary faces.
A line on a graph.
A linear relationship: dullness in the day.
Eight hours.
Still chasing.
The same seat.
Same. Same. Same.
Same stick.

Straight lines. Same lines.
Caught the clock.
5 o'clock.
False hope.
Lost grip.
Lost hope.
So, we simply sip.

a constant noise; a continual path
the roads are full, and we are all stuck in
TRAFFIC

we rush
rush hour
rush day
rush year
rush life
rushing our lives
rushing our time
away

Step.

Step.

100.
200.
300.

FAT.

You were born to be better than that.

GALLERY

An art gallery in which, you cannot make sense.
Following the next right.
Just to realise there is nothing left.
Stare. Staring. Stare.
Pushing too hard.
You pull away your care.

Distorting mirrors.
A carnival inside.
Misleading your movement.
A fun house; no slide.

Processed in the brain.
Received by the eye.
Dazed.
Information you read; is it a lie?

Opticians are convinced.
Normality in sight.

This is an optical illusion.
This is life.

The hazard sign on a bottle.
Symbolic of the word toxic.
We grow up warned of the word toxic.

Chemicals surround us.
All causing great harm.
Left unaware, there is greater damage than a needle in our arm.

There is a chemical in our brain.
Which hits directly to the heart.

Leaving scar tissue, excruciating pain.
On a day when it is sunny, you constantly feel rain.
Very misleading, disguised until too late.
Every cell in your body, a chemical can manipulate.

Dopamine.
Euphoria.
Adrenaline.
Dead.

SOMETHING

Not even a pause
where there is nothing
still nothing
is something
so
this time is not nothing.

Silence
is a sound
played to a universal
crowd.

Pause   pause   pause
The time between the words
the time
the gap
makes silence worse.

Conceptualise
the world
before we appear.

Would we acknowledge
the hum in our ear?

He retains it all to his

l
e
f
t
.

The entirety of his being.
Seeing
eating
breathing
left.

                                        To be on the right.
Is so unheard.
Right.
Is to be alright.
Right.
He is not right.

Left.
Why the left?
Triggered in his mind.

The

l

e

f

t

.

His father left.
He is now left.

Every day, the same.

the same the same the same the same

My eyelids peel open and in that moment,
I realise, I am awake.
Fuck my fucking life.
So, what am I going to do today?
Well, absolutely nothing that I said I was going to do.
That is what.

It feels like I am stuck under a bus. Under a wheel of a bus. The weight pushing me further down that I wish the floor would swallow me up. One big gulp and I could disappear.

gulp. food. what can i eat today?

…

you know the answer. nothing.

ONE

One
One Two One
One Two Three Two One
One Two Three Four Three Two One
One
It started with one
It was the first one
Now the next one
Now one; is gone.

One
Has
Won.

* * *

INITIATION

D
r
i
p

it starts with a drip.
You are wishing for the hot,
yet it starts off cold.
Slowly, very slowly.
Heating up with every drip.

ITCH

It is a gradual tickle.
The itch on your arm.
A travelling rash.
Where no eyes will see the harm.

Eczema in the mind.
Unable to catch; unable to find.

With eyes sealed shut.
It is all you can see.
Taunting.
No amount of glue, will disclose me.

A vampire in the face.
Feeding on your thoughts.
Slow nibbles periodically.
Each pathway; feeble as straw.

The more you scratch.
The blood will rise.
There is so much more than the rash.
Physically seen by the eyes.

Eyes.
Eyes see.
Eyes see you.
I see you.

I see your eyes.
Your eyes.
Your eyes see me.

Eye.
I see you,
seeing me.

<u>HIM</u>

Maybe one day she will look you in the eyes, smile, say 'I am okay' and mean it. Maybe one day she will look at you, and stare back at you with those big brown eyes, and look at you, seeing you. You notice the freckle in her eye, like you are admiring the countries on the globe. You notice the sun meeting the side of her face and hair, so gentle and soft. She's glowing.

HESITATION

New Year's Eve.
Never wanting to leave.
The countdown begins.
3.. 2.. 1.
1
it only takes one.
Yes.
No.
Wait.
I do not know.
question
question
Pulled in; suck me in.
Given in.

I am in.

ALIVE

A round you.
L ook around.
It is exquisite.
Virtual reality.
Everything is beautiful.

You are alive.

it was a drunken dance
led by sinking smiles
the blurred beat
in our enchanted eyes.

mischief and movement
music and medication

the rhythm took us together
to the world of relaxation

INSANE

tell me about your thoughts
open the gate into your brain
unlock the undisclosed safe
i want to feel your body's insane

TRANCE

Words.
Your words
are my
fixation.

I am left
you leave me
bewildered in
fascination.

Hear
hear your voice
a soothing melody from the
drum.

Wait
wait for you
waiting all day for you to
come.

I think it was the way her voice said my name.
Like when you first hear a song and play it over again.

Her music was her words.
Every beat made me melt.
Almost like a lullaby.
I cannot live without.

I leave her on repeat, for nothing can compare.
I hear the keys on the piano, when she leans to tie her hair.

A symphony of love.
A tone full of lust.
Soon became an album, sold with words that I can trust.

If you can hear the beat within your lucky ear,
instantly you will know,
know that she is near.

HYPNOTISE

You stay on repeat
every day
every week.
Your words branded
in my mind,
I am hypnotised
I've forgotten how to speak.

SINK

Sink
i
n
g

We are falling
deeper.
We are now in this
hole.

HIM

The simple thought of living a second of my life without her is enough to drive me into an eternal ruin. The simplicity in her beauty, so pure and young. I am bewildered by her. A life of experience held in such a fragile flower. Fighting on its own. I love her. Why can't she see herself through my eyes? She would see the way people's faces light up, the fairy lights in their eyes when her lips spread across her face. She makes people happy. Everyone except herself.

STRANGER

We spoke like storytellers.
Reading aloud.
'The Tale of Us…'
Distracted, easy to forget.
Two strangers on the bus.

TRUTH IN NUMBERS

6 months old, I cried as my mother made me eat.
16 years old, I do the same.

3 years.
3 years old turned to 3 years young.
Running around I was always hot.
3 years on, I am nothing but cold.

10x10= 100.
100 too many.
But you cannot make a pound, if you only have one penny.

1 pound.
There is never enough.
1 pound is always ideal.
Still for me there is too much.

STARS

The stars not captured by our eyes at night
although too far, beam twice as bright.

Take a trip into your garden, stare up into the air.
You will see one common constellation
convinced you know all that is there.

In the path between the conjoining of our stars
our paths got cast astray.
Distance may have grown, greatness may be hidden
I will still shine for you
every
day

CITY NIGHT

There is something about this city at night.

Those beady eyes will catch you out.
You are the deer.
You have no idea.
Continuous ring of fire.
A circus on the street.
Glazing over.
Mesmerised.
Awoke by the sound of a beep.

You are seeing.
And unseeing.
You do not know what is hidden.
Short cut alleyway.
Now forbidden.
Once there in the day.
Gone by night.
Your eyes become distracted.
Vast amounts.
Bright lights.

The world falls dark.
The sun, asleep.
Borrowing its life,
to the posts on the street.

<u>UP</u>

I am so completely okay.
I am ordinary.
It is inadequate.
Waste of my ti…

Pound.
Pound.
Pound.

Pounding so much I feel like a millionaire. In my heart. My chest. The DJ has spun me around. Dizziness of the deck.

My head blown off my neck.

* * *

EXPERIMENTATION

That moment you realise it is not enough.
Now stuck in a trance of what it could be.
Turn up the power,
increasing intensity.
Feel the sensation.

A heavy head.

Weighted waves of thought.

Muscles of the mind.

A tide where you are caught.

Power

in your perspective.

Strength

so deceptive.

Silently, seeing.

Bravely, being.

HIM

North. East. South. West.
I dream to travel the world.

At first, I saw the globe.
Immediately I knew.
The tide has sucked me in.
Waves holding me like glue.

Then I watched the wind.
Constant movement in the air.
On different days; different speeds.
Different rhythms through each hair.

At last I saw the desert.
Vast amounts of soft, bright sand.
When too hot; will burn the skin.
Yet it will never burn my hand.

I can grasp the mountains.
The first one to discover.
The range across your chest.
Each one taller than the other.

The stars on your cheeks.
The islands on your hips.

A world I know unlike the rest.
A world I will travel at my best.
North. East. South. West.

ROLL

It rolled off the tongue and into my eyes. A hill with bladed words. Words shooting out like sharp blades of grass. Rolling. Rolling. Rolling. I can see them rolling. Directly towards me. I will stand still. My feet are stuck in set. I want your words to hit me. Knock me down if you can.

There is no line. I cannot see an end. Inexistent in my sight. Maybe it is just the hope. Hope. Hope that your words will roll infinitely. I would rather, much rather, have your words. Rotation of your mouth. I would rather have the rotation in your mouth; than the rotation on my watch.

Time. Timeless. You are timeless. Unaware of the time; for my time is now yours. My sight is impaired. Your haze is now mine.

A last penny. Now gone. I would give it all for you.
I would never spend a penny.
To spend all my time with you.

ART

Let me envelope your body
from your head to your toes.
I've never known lust until
I took off your clothes.
Your body is art
art worth a prize.
Tell me how you like
my drawing on your thighs.
Feel the brush of my paint
sinking all through your skin.
Come collect your art at my door
I'll be waiting to let you in.

SCENT

Think of the scent that reminds you of home.
Lingering on your jumper, making it your own.
Embraced in your arms, can you sense me?
I am intoxicated by your smell.
Flying like a honey bee.

You have freshened my air.
All it took was one spray.
A singular droplet.
That accidentally flew my way.

It feels so… right.
My body is feeling dizzy.
I'm losing all my sight.

SUN

You became my sun.
Your eyes became my rise and set.
I'd watch them open
then close.
An illumination
you cannot forget.

Intrigued.
The pupils in your eyes,
darker than the skies.
To me they were my light,
looking at me
you make my world so
bright.

I've lost the feel of the sun
for you are now my source of heat.
To feel the light and heat you give

on my body
for my body

is such a
fiery
forceful
treat.

BLIND

Love me
wisely.

Craft your movement
with the pierced pencil
lightly.

You fill my sight
with your body
my eyes are falling
blindly.

Conscious
I am falling in love
with you
ever so
slightly.

REALISATION

That's how I know I loved him. When the dice rolled to end in my corrupt game of hurt. Corrupt.

My multi-player game that only I knew we were playing.

I knew I loved him, when I couldn't hurt him.

I knew I loved him when I chased him down the rabbit hole instead of weighing him down to push myself up. Crocodiles drowned in waterfalls as manipulative tears turned to cries for his love.

I, turns to him as his words become addictive and all I hear is him.

I am feeling. Feeling safe.

A dark room filled with strobe lights; still all I see is him.

Unlocking the key to fuel our night; licking the sugar from our fingers as we dare miss a bite.

We dance.

It's all a bit blurry; still all I see is him.

He sends arrows to my spine, to my knees, as his hands twine with mine.

Mine. He is mine.

We lose sight of ourselves but still hold sight of each other.

The first layer of our love may be covered in white sand but the concrete above is so solid, so pure.

We sink deeper.

Words adrift in the night. We laughed, a lot.

Two sheets of glass reflect beams so big that the smiles are contagious.
We still laugh. Even more.

His body I crave. His soul, I need.
He is out for the day. Leftover turkey in the fridge.
Longing, longing, longing.
Without him I have withdrawal.

He is back, his bag packed ready for us to escape.
Yet, reality seems better when looking at his face.
Let's stay, stay here.

Looking into his eyes all I see is the sclera.
Looking at his skin all I see is the colour.
Everyday spent airborne to be left stuck in a cloud.
Still, he is my parachute.

From a stop at a platform turned to a direct train.
Taking speed fast.
Flashing. So fast I cannot keep up.
He's left me on the platform but still holds his bag.

Yet, he calls me half way.
A voice so soothing, taking me home in his first word.
The jealousy feels stupid.
Transformed to relief that his journey was safe.

He's home. My home.
Up close the windows are cracked.
Unlocked; the latch at the back.
Someone has broken in. Broke into his mind.
Still when he is with me, he is safe.
He is mine.

'I am sorry.' He says and forever, I do not mind.

i do not even need my fingers anymore. you already make me sick. it makes me laugh, how do you still believe me when i say that i am sorry? i am not sorry. the only sorry emotion i make sense of in my body is the pity i feel as i watch your pathetic attempts repeating again. i am hollow. you are stuck. stuck caring. stop caring.

SHE SLEEPS

The lights turned off.
They turn their backs.
A wall erupts.
The bed seems cracked.

She turns to me.
I am wearing her skin.
The air cannot breathe.
No space within.

Love seems forgotten.
Goodnight, a forgotten word.
Separate sides in separate dreams.
A world she finds absurd.

Without fail; every night.
She whispers velvet into my ear.
Two bodies mould to one.
Feeling safe when I am near.

It may just be my hand on hers.
Or my foot sleeping on her thigh.
The knowledge of her; grasping for my body.
Is an addictive, unimaginable high.

HE SLEEPS

A safety blanket. His leg is my shield. Lay over my body; bicep in my hand. He nourishes me with warmth. His warmth. My hand cups his chin as if we are sculptures in France. The kiss. His kiss.

Drowsiness overcomes dizziness. Held steady in those arms. Spiders running up our arms; tickles until we feel the calm. A tap of the receptor. Bodies melted in the cold. He is the comfort. He turns my pillow into stone. Flesh filled with feathers. A body. A home.

* * *

REGULATION

The water is heating.
Your senses are alive.
With every drip, you can sense it.
That is why it is so endearing.
You have full control.

Or so you think.

DOODLE

A game that you play.
Getting high is the aim.

Up
Up
Up

On the platform, you jump.
Personal best.
Still not enough.
Weight on.
Platform gone.
Dissolving away.
Restart… Play.

Leaning on people should be sought with great care.
Leaning too hard; disappeared into air.

BUMP

I heard it.
A distinguishable sound.
The hum of people in my ear; I heard your chime in the crowd.
A chime. A clang. A crash.

It was only a bump.

Ha.
Too right you are.
A bump.

I cannot do it anymore. I want to go. Please just make it go away. I am not living. I am dying. I am being killed. The murderer is close. Closer than they know. Do not come too close. I will hurt you.

. . .

Why did I do it again?

TEAR

At first it was a tear in the wall, to my heart.
When the loved weighed down the bricks, we were smitten from the start.

Then the barriers we enclosed in, each began to tear.
Every minute hidden flaw, inhaling the same air.

Surprisingly, a tear in our nightmares and fears.
Every soothing, calming word, trickled like syrup in our ears.

Unexpectedly around the corner; a car tears through the trust.
A road where paranoia and lies are a must.

Now we are left with a tear in the muscles, mainly the heart.
As the heart broke much quicker than the wall at the start.

The car has now crashed when the road became unclear.
Now every tear, has turned to a tear.

I cannot help her.
I cannot do it.

I cannot help him.
I cannot do it.

WHY CAN I NOT HELP HER
PLEASE LET ME HELP HER.

WHY CAN I NOT HELP HIM
PLEASE LET ME HELP HIM.

I am here for you, I would die for you. But something tells me you will be the one to die first. The sadness fills my heart. Sadness that will never go away. Filling every single cell of my body, stealing the oxygen from my lungs and the blood from my veins. If my love was an injection, you will always find an oxygen bubble to murder it. Spending your whole life waiting for that one lethal injection. My love. You were mine. Now you are moving to the hands of a new lover. I cannot compete with the love that you feel from your illness.

Unacquainted love.

WAR

There is a war out here
worse than bullets and bombs.
It is much more excruciating
so discrete with its danger.

So simple at the start.
The simplicity ends up being the worse part.

Looking back at how it was
in comparison to how it has been.

Stare into his face.
Consider his soul.
Accept the love you feel.
Still know his is not real.

The dire feeling of letting go.
As they become the one person
you wish
you did not know.

SHOT

A bullet will not hide the guilt.
Vodka cannot seize the pain.
Injections do not forever numb the pain.
A throw does not always make aim.

Put it down to trust
blame it on luck.
You will stay where you are
if you
give up.

LAUGH

Humour me.
Amuse me.
Fill me to the top.
Standing up.
You are lying down.
Lying.
Lies.
Overflown.
A brain overflown with lies.

How you think I am unaware.
Under the light.
You think.
I am stuck in the dark.
Stuck…
Like you.

<u>*HIM*</u>

Is it cruel?
A cruel mistress.
Beauty.
No cruelty.
At least; I make myself believe.
She holds out her hand.
Jerking back when I reach to hold.
Watches with glee; when I fall into her hole.
Crying.
She laughs.
Crying… Lying.

Intelligence.
Profound knowledge.
This scheme in her head.
She knows her steps.
Step by step.

She is gliding.
On your waves of tears.
She is riding.

CHILD-HOOD

Childhood
Adulthood
Taught to cross the road
when we see the hood.

Childhood phase
now an adulthood craze.
Far too in depth
stuck in the game
only one life
remains.

POLAR

you came like winter
sharp
frozen time
the world around me fell silent
snow starts to fall
falling so delicately

you left me
cold
numb
my world is now
ice age.

SNOW

I used to like winter.
I was fond of the cold.

Dreamed of bonfires.
Wished for snowflakes.

'You need a boyfriend for the winter...'

Turns out they only ruin a season.
When the flames run out and it is snowing for no reason.
The snow stops falling. Flying up his nose.
The flames stop rising. Falling into ash down his throat.

Now I cannot dream of winter.
I can only dream of how to win.
Fighting a losing battle.
Every day spent fighting for him.

HIM

She tells me she loves me. I know she does not. She could not even if she tried. Still, I am still here, clinging on to any piece of hope there is. If I was to see her fall, I would fall. If she was to see me fall, she would walk. Such a beautiful walk.

I watch as global warming floods the earth as the countries disappear. You watch the sun burn her hair as it begins to disappear.

She is going to disappear.

ALMOST

1mm
away from winning your heart.
So close, still so far
now I am beyond the start.

2nd
place.
Almost won the race.
The day our paths crossed,
synonym of almost…
I
lost.

A cunning never-ending game.
When did you become a sport?
With rules, much more deceiving than
I thought.

HUMAN NATURE

It was a slow, very slow process. Half the time I did not even realise it was happening. It was. The whole time it was happening; in front of my eyes. The scales became outweighed. Along with the smile on his face. The curve turned straight, then the straight became a slant.
He had blinked away any life in his eyes. He was hollow. Not even a tree; but a branch on the floor. Teeth grasp the branch as the dog runs away. He is unfamiliar. He is far away.
The dog barks. His bark falls off.
Leaving me with less. Less of him.

An overweighed parcel. A suitcase filled too high.
He proceeded to take the extra weight and keep it by his side.
The weight goes in. The weight falls off.
I could not feel the breeze.
It was only until the storm.
Coincidental.
A droplet of rain feels just like my tears.

The storm is inside. The storm is inside my head. Internal rain pours, heaviness of my head. Power has risen. A power trip in his mind.
He created the wind which blew the clouds my way. He watched as they fell.
He watched as they flood. My body began to drown.
He silently stood.
Barriers around my mind so the water cannot pour out.
He is left dry. He does not cry.

Unnatural human nature.
Manmade weather.
A worthless weatherman.
Manipulative and clever.

<u>SHOP</u>

In this shop, full of people;
you stood out on the shelf.
The shoes you want but cannot afford.
Now cannot stop thinking about.

I have wandered about trying you on.
How your arms may feel on mine.
Too big?
Too tight?
Too long?
Too short?
Worth more money than I can afford.

I can stare into the mirror and not see myself.
A ghost of my drained heart.

I knew you did not suit me.
I should have left you on the shelf.
For the love, I felt, has drawn me out.

After wearing a top, you cannot take it back.
After breaking a heart, you cannot mend the crack.

FLICK

Flicker.
Flicked.
Flick.
Your eyes are flickering.

Flicked a switch.
Losing breath.
You are creating a stitch.

Your hands are curled up.
Like a sleeping cat.
But the cat is out the bag.
Disguise came off with your hat.

You are tensing
I am afraid
you ignore my tears
you
left me betrayed.

You are not who you say
you are not you
gaping
glaring
one single thought
…
Who?

WHERE

are you there?

there was a response
but it was not
you.

the body of you
the bygone of you
i am searching
observing
wishing
for you.

missing posters
pointless
for your body is still
here.
your mind is elsewhere
elsewhere
where
where have you gone?

LIE

A page filled with words.

Dictionary.

Defining your dialect.

Your words are undefined.

Your words are not followed.

With your words,

comes no purpose.

Searching through a dictionary of lies.

I find

compulsive

addictive

a-dick-tive

a dickhead.

* * *

ADDICTION

I have danced my whole life.
Paid more money than I own.

It seems a great pity;
only dancing with death makes me feel known.

CLOSING

Red.
Upon us.
Fast.
Lights.
Red.

An explosion. In your mind.
Social immensities. Come to life.
You are in.
In another world.
A dimension
of speed and light.
As the planets on the ceiling
bring the bodies to life.

Step   Step

Madness.
Moving.
Reality is blurred.
The crowd is grooving.
A rush.
A ride.
Finding the perfect place to hide.
Mesmerised.
Indescribable circus.
Bodies upon bodies.
The feeling of us.

ERASER

Mattress please open.
Swallow me up.
Open your seams.
My body has had enough.

Can you not hear it scream?

Closing my eyes.
My brain is stuck.
Stuck in this race.
Dreaming of how this word
could now forget my face.

Is it possible?
To disappear.

My sole reason I am staying;
the ones I hold near.

The memory of myself.
Wondering how I can erase.

Is there a rubber for my body?

Let me OUT.

Of this cruel maze.

TENSE

Sweating and shivering.
Frozen in the heat.
Pulsating. Hit a wall.
Now silent in the sheets.
Memories of what you have done.
Reminder in your mouth.
Creeping out of your discoloured lips.
A bubble bath.
The soap is bleach.
Turned whiter than your poison.
An endless love affair.

Except.
The bath you soak in.
Is getting too hot.
Evaporating.
Shallow.

It
is
heavy.

Weighing your eyes d
o
w
n
.
Compulsion.
Confusion.
Comatose.

The breath is now stopping.
Abusive air in your nose.

MODERN LOVE

The same hand.
You have it.
You have
faulty fingerprint recognition
A different
feel
touch.

Eyes
eye
I do not.

Not
no more
not anymore.

I do not love you.
Not anymore.

You know all the answers, but you know how to act.
The words are written, and the roles are rehearsed.
A face forgotten under the face of another.

You know, *I know.*

MASK

I know the face under the mask
maybe
definitely
even better
than I know my own reflection.

Masking my feelings to the face of the mask.

I know
but
I cannot say no.

FLYING

Do you believe in you heart that it will stop the pain?
Because it will not.
It will only pause for another day.

You are absorbing it in; to create an escape.
Whilst pushing you further into the debris it creates.

S haking.
T ossing.
O ver.
P ulse.

Over

d
o
s
e

are you free?

h
i
g
h

LYING

There is no sweet seduction,
in the way you take me to bed.
For my bed
is lies.
Staring past
your eyes.

Every time I say it back,
the bones in my body
disappear
one by one.
They are lying down
out of your site
for I am
lying.

I know the path of the veins,
in your eyes.
The shade, the dullness, the size.

I had never noticed before,
that was the moment I knew.
I was looking at them.
Not into them.
Lying when I say I love you.

see her eyes

captivating

her mind

calculating

her soul

capturing

now your body

crippling

her control

rippling

a mind left

paralysed

fatal venom in

her eyes

and I do not know
if I am desperately wishing
to forget you
or feel you again

* * *

PERCEPTION

Ignite.
Insecurities.
Inside.
In my eyes.

the first word

goodbye

the first word that I took back

my stolen words

now mine again

goodbye to the thief

goodbye

at last

BRICKS

It hit me like a ton of
Smashed by a ton of

A series of amnesia
memory still frail.

BED

How selfish of me to lie in pity on that bed.
Opposite a bruised angel; lost hair on her head.
Her cries are real; an unimaginable feel.
Guilt stricken.
In good health.
A world in which, in the bed, she dreams about.
Their attention is on me.
She is waiting in the line.
Cruel; I am cruel.

Stop wasting her time.

WHO

Who wants a
DYING
child
friend
sibling
lover?

When they could
swiftly
fall
into the
living arms
of another?

<u>DAY</u>

Yesterday was spent agonizing about tomorrow.
A misspent day.
Frittered away.

Epiphany.
Finally.

Today is yesterday's tomorrow.
Dwelling on the past.
Prioritise acceptance.
The day will start to last.

you have a problem

No.
Normal.
Normality.
Reality.

Oh.
Ok.
OKAY.
No way.

Pardon.
Persevere.
Perhaps.
Relapse.

We are opaque, we cannot see under our skin.

There is no transparency to what we hold inside.

Guess work.

Our experimentation has created wounds to be healed.

Open the wounds to disinfect your thoughts.

A wound will soon be a scar.

Replacements of tissue that touched any tears you cried.

Your fear; I can feel it.

'There is no greater fear than fear itself.' '

There is something greater.

You are greater.

HEAL

Such an enrapturing shoe; broken heel.
An extraordinary bag; faulty seal.
A Michelin star; unarrived meal.
A breath-taking building; starting to keel.

and just like you;
they need to
heal.

RACE

it takes a while to realise
refusal to see through our own eyes
one
there will only ever be
one

face and body
love and accept
no one can
reset

these people paying for change
all fall in steps behind
for every day in pain
is a precious waste of time.

FIRST

A lingering smell.
Old plastic and dust.
Stale.
Cigarettes and coffee.
No end to a circle.
The chance to go around again.
Is a biscuit as sweet as the residual sugar?
Twitch. Shake. Tap. Stare.
Distant people. Breathing the same stale air.

He is new. You can tell.
Face is red. Eyes are down.
Welcome to our circle.
Lending my ear to his melancholy words.

Leaning back.
My eyelids begin to greet.
Buzz. Buzz. Buzzing.
Same old shit.

Snatch. Trap.
Another; pointless catch.
Contempt with getting by.
A foolish belief.
A bird stuck in a tree… so high.

DRIVE

Who is driving those trees?
Speeding down the lane.
One lane.
A one-way road.
They proceed on the route.

A sudden halt.
All the bodies still in sight.
The trees are now statues.

Or maybe…
Just maybe.

The tree is motionless.

You are the motion.
You are the increase in

                      rate
                      speed
                      tempo.

SPA

Trapped in
solitude.

Lost in earth's
safari.

Unsure of where to
search.

Making air our
sanctum.

Finding peace with every
step

Pondering
ponder
where this path will lead us
next.

<u>WASTE</u>

A waste of hurt.
When love is a lie.
I do not need this hurt.
There are too many blue skies.

So many green trees.
Power cells of the earth.
I am... alive.
I have been since birth.

<u>CLOUD</u>

Moving with high speed.
Next day,
Stood so still.
Some days unnoticed.
We examine their shapes,
staring at their beautiful body form.
Underrated.
People forget that they can hide the sun.
An illuminous star,
hidden by white.

Appreciate the white.
Such an intriguing, unique sight.

FREE

Provided with life. A gift from the dark. Despite the reputation.
It forgives what we all say. Forgiving. Far too forgiving.

Raining down. A sacrifice for life.
Selfish. We are. We moan. We hate.
Life is handed to us. A free plate.
Still, here we are. Glasses filled with hate.

Kindness taken for weakness. Hidden power.
Medicinal shower. Misused hour.
Content. A desirable feeling.
Would not be possible. Without the dark. In need of healing.

The tears are the rain. What is life without pain?
The sun will free from the cloud. The rain will stop falling so loud.

It is from the dark again.
That I grow and educate.
My beautiful brain.

ENGLISH ROSE

'Red hair, pastel skin, blushed cheeks.
You really are an English rose.'

I imagine that is his way of saying that I am beautiful.
As a rose is a flower metaphorical of beauty.
Perceptively, I see it.
The soft, so soft, petals.
Sending a divine smell, received by your air ways.

Yet I will not fall for that
you should have been more clever.
You know just as well
roses do not last forever.

What happens when the petals dry?
When the enchantress ages?
Seductress is no more.
when petal by petal
they fall to the
floor.

I can see the paths, that flow through your mind.
Your eyes open the gate.
When my petals are gone and you have seen all that I own.
You will not stay around, I will not call you home.

Half-hearted attempts to see my beauty.
No divulgence to see into my mind.
Next time say that she is your oak tree.
So many wise leaves
the greatest one you will find.

15

RIBBON

After a day too, many.
Lost count of many cracks.
The bull charging through my brain.
Finally, is held back.

Using the scissors that we hold.
We cut the ribbon.
Imperfect. Still in two.
Now I fold the ribbon into a bow.
To wrap your present; as I thank you.

Prioritising a promise to yourself.

Everything is falling into place.

Except,

nothing is falling.

Nothing will fall as you will climb everyday.

Defined.

You have redefined your mind.

SERENITY

34486159R00060

Printed in Great Britain
by Amazon